MAKING THE MOST OF

Outdoor Learning

Linda Thor
nton

Featherstone

Published 2011 by Featherstone Education
Bloomsbury Publishing plc
50 Bedford Square, London WC1B 3DP
www.acblack.com

ISBN 978-1-4081-372-91

Text © Pat Brunton and Linda Thornton 2011
Design © Bob Vickers 2011

A CIP record for this publication is available from the British Library.

Printed in Great Britain by Latimer Trend & Company Limited

This book is produced using paper that is made from wood grown in
managed, sustainable forests. It is natural, renewable and recyclable.
The logging and manufacturing processes conform to the environmental
regulations of the country of origin.

To see our full range of titles visit **www.acblack.com**

Contents

Acknowledgements

Our thanks go to the staff, children and parents of:

Reflections Nursery, Worthing, West Sussex.

Lincolnshire Montessori Nursery and School, Caistor, Lincolnshire.

Oak House Nursery School, Ross-on-Wye.

St Breock Primary School, Wadebridge, Cornwall.

Portheyl Children's Centre, Cornwall.

Photographs courtesy of:

alc associates
Staff at Reflections Nursery
Lincolnshire Montessori Nursery and School
Oak House Nursery School
Lisa Branson
Sarah Wickett
Reflections on Learning

Introduction

The *Making the Most of* series has been specially written in order to share good practice, showing what high quality learning and development for young children looks like in real settings. The scenarios described in this book all focus on the use of the outdoor environment to demonstrate the exciting opportunities which arise when practitioners observe closely children's self-initiated play and look for the 'extraordinary' in the 'ordinary'.

The role of the practitioner in these child-initiated learning experiences was to provide interesting and unusual resources for the children to explore. The children were then given time to be creative, to try out their ideas, to satisfy their curiosity and to become absorbed in the 'serious business of play'. Practitioners paid close attention to what the children were doing and saying and documented their learning in photographs, written observations and transcripts of the conversations. This provided a wealth of information on which to base individual assessments about where to take each child next in order to consolidate and extend their learning and development.

The outdoor environments described, and what happens within them, vary from short term experiences taking place in the outdoor area of a setting, to examples of longer term projects involving planned visits or, in some instances Forest School experiences. The emphasis throughout is on seeing the potential of any outdoor environment as a place which can enhance and enrich young children's learning experiences.

From reading the scenarios described in this book it is hoped that practitioners will:

- Consider new ways of building on the interests and fascinations of the children they work with.
- Extend the range of environments, resources and equipment available to young children.
- Explore the use of photographs and transcripts of children's conversations as the basis for planning what opportunities to offer children next.

Each of the scenarios has been presented within the context of the areas of learning in the revised Early Years Foundation Stage (EYFS). However, young children take a holistic approach to learning and it is easy to see that in any one scenario there are connections to many different areas of learning. By the same token, although connections have been made in this book to the EYFS, the statements about children's learning and development are applicable to any curriculum guidance or framework.

How this book is structured

The book is divided into six sections that relate to the seven areas of learning and development in the revised EYFS:

- Personal, Social and Emotional Development (PSED)
- Physical Development (PD)
- Communication and Language, Literacy (CL, L)
- Mathematics (M)
- Understanding the World (UW)
- Expressive Arts and Design (EAD)

Each section is made up of four different scenarios with accompanying photographs which include:

- An environment for . . . How to use the outdoor environment with children of all ages to engage their curiosity, broaden their experience and develop their skills and knowledge.
- Two illustrated examples of children's experiences in the outdoor area of a setting that highlight the role of the practitioner in supporting children's learning and development.
- Further afield . . . An example of the benefits of organising experiences which take children further afield, into an urban or a rural environment.

Many of the experiences described in this book have happened in a nursery that draws its inspiration from the Reggio Approach to early years education and care. A significant feature of the Reggio Approach is the attention paid to the quality of the environments which young children encounter and the influence that these have on their learning. This is explained in more detail in the first scenario of each section of this book.

The scenarios illustrate how the principles of the EYFS are put into practice in real life situations. The text has deliberately been kept short and succinct to encourage the reader to look closely at the photographs and think about the learning and development that they can see taking place.

Each scenario contains:

- **In the EYFS:** links to particular aspects of the revised EYFS.
- **Starting points:** a description of the context of the experience and any resources used.
- **Learning and development:** an illustrated snapshot of good practice in the EYFS.
- **Other things to try:** additional ideas on the same theme that you can use to provoke further investigation and development.

Valuing the outdoor environment

Young children benefit in many ways from being out of doors all year round, and, therefore, in all weathers. Whilst in many early years settings children have access to the outdoors throughout the year, there are some practitioners who have a less positive view of children being out in all weathers. For everyone, it's important to realise that playing outside should not be restricted to warm, dry weather – late autumn, winter and early spring each present their own unique opportunities for learning. Practitioners who have a positive attitude to being out of doors will not only enjoy the experience themselves, but will foster a sense of pleasure in the children as they explore and play together. To ensure that everyone gets the most out of their outdoor experiences it's important to provide suitable clothing and footwear – for adults as well as children!

Being outside gives babies and young children first-hand experience of the weather, the seasons and the natural world. The outdoor environment offers children opportunities to do different things and to do familiar things on a larger scale and with less concern about noise levels. Playing outside gives babies and young children the freedom to explore using all their senses, to use their bodies and to have fun.

Making the most of outdoor spaces such as gardens or the local park will give young children the opportunities they need to explore and discover, to express themselves and to relive their experiences through their natural language of movement. The freedom to play outside, build a den, climb a tree, play hide and seek or chase, enjoy singing and action games or draw with chalks on a paved area are all wonderful ways of helping children to develop self-confidence and to learn their own physical limits in a safe environment.

It's also important that practitioners work with parents to help them to understand the value of playing outside in terms of their children's learning and development, their wellbeing and their physical and mental health. In addition to explaining to parents the 'whys' and 'hows' of outdoor play in your setting, you could share some of the ideas in this book to help them see the benefits of exploring the great outdoors with their children.

Following young children's interests and ideas

Evidence shows that young children often possess sophisticated thinking skills and creativity which may not at first be recognised or valued by practitioners and family members. Early years practitioners have the challenging task of creating emotional and physical environments, indoors and out of doors, in which very young children can flourish, displaying their emerging interests and abilities. Practitioners do this best when they . . .

- create rich and exciting learning environments full of open-ended resources which children can use to explore their own particular interests and fascinations.
- provide a supportive framework in which children have the time, space and resources to follow their own ideas.
- are able to feel comfortable with the uncertainty of not knowing what's going to happen next.
- observe closely the children they work with, noticing and acknowledging their ideas and paying attention to the things which interest them.
- listen attentively to the ideas and feelings which children communicate, verbally and non-verbally, and respond appropriately, supporting and extending children's developing knowledge, skills and understanding.
- challenge children to reflect on and explain their ideas, encouraging higher level thinking skills.
- communicate well with parents and carers, sharing information and gathering as complete a picture as possible about the children they work with.

Managing physical risk

If we try to remove all possible risk from children's lives there is a danger that we will inhibit rather than extend their learning. Some dangers clearly have to be avoided and we would be failing in our duty of care to young children if we did not protect them from these hazards. In other situations it is important to assess the real risk presented by, for example, exploring in the garden after dark, a well planned visit to the local park or corner shop, using a hammer or a saw or climbing on to a fallen tree trunk. Children are entitled to experiences of this type to broaden their understanding of how to manage in the real world in which they live. Adopting a risk/benefit approach to assessing experiences of this type provides the opportunity to evaluate the benefits of any experience in relation to its potential risks. If the benefits outweigh the risks it would be appropriate to find a way to make the experience happen.

Spending time explaining to children what makes some activities potentially dangerous and demonstrating how to behave safely will be far more beneficial to their long term learning than simply banning or avoiding particular situations. Our ultimate aim should be to help children master the skills they need to manage risk and danger for themselves. Children given the opportunity to experience this type of 'risky freedom' will grow in competence and self-confidence as they master a wide range of physical and social skills.

Good risk assessment will take into account the expectations of the adults, the age of the children, the nature of the activity, the physical environment and the degree of supervision required. Activities which present children with risk and challenge can then go ahead on the clear understanding that small accidents or mishaps that occur are part of the learning experience for everyone.

Health and safety on visits and outings

Careful planning and preparation are the keys to the success of any excursion beyond the early years setting. Children, practitioners and parents all need to have a shared understanding of what is expected of them to make exploring the outdoor environment safe and enjoyable.

For staff this involves careful thought about the purpose of the visit and a detailed consideration of safety issues. Parents and carers need to prepare the children by ensuring they are appropriately dressed for the experience and are enthusiastic about the prospect of being out of doors. Children need to be aware of the importance of following instructions and behaving in a sensible manner.

The best way to take account of all these considerations is to produce a policy for using the outdoor environment that is written in consultation with staff, children, parents and carers.

Things to consider when drawing up your policy:

1. The reasons why you want children to explore the local environment including links to areas of children's learning and development.

2. How you will comply with statutory regulations regarding organisation and safety. For example:
   - Staffing ratios must meet at least the minimum statutory levels for children of different ages. You may wish to exceed these by using volunteers who are fully aware of your safety policy and procedures.
   - Identifying staff roles and responsibilities, ensuring that they are experienced and suitably qualified and are familiar with the local environment and the route they will be taking.
   - Systems for logging who has gone on the visit, the route, time of departure, expected time of return.
   - Strategies for ensuring the safe control of children while out walking, such as holding hands, walking sensibly, staying together as a group and listening to instructions.
   - Including children with disabilities.
   - Equipment, such as buggies and prams should be in good repair and fit for their purpose.
   - Staff should take with them a first aid kit, a mobile phone and drinking water.

3. How you will give information to parents and gain their consent to take children out into the wider environment beyond the setting.

4. Arrangements for staff training and professional development covering topics ranging from first aid, road safety and behaviour management to Forest School training.

5. Guidance on appropriate clothing for different weather conditions.

An environment for Personal, Social and Emotional Development

In the EYFS

The following statements are taken from the Learning and Development requirements of the EYFS, Personal, Social and Emotional Development.

Help children to:

- Develop a positive sense of themselves and others.
- Form positive relationships and develop respect for others.
- Develop social skills and learn how to manage their feelings.
- Understand appropriate behaviour in groups.
- Have confidence in their own abilities.

Starting points

Many early years settings in the UK have been influenced by the work of the infant-toddler centres and pre-schools of Reggio Emilia in northern Italy where the environment, both indoors and outside, plays an active role in determining how children play and learn.

By carefully planning the outdoor environment, early years practitioners are able to enhance their provision for children's personal, social and emotional development. In a day nursery in the south of England, practitioners have endeavoured to create spaces outside, as well as indoors, where children can:

- develop relationships
- explore and investigate
- communicate
- have privacy
- be creative
- make choices

Learning and development

Places for developing relationships
The outdoor area of a nursery has a variety of enclosed small spaces for the children to enjoy. Practitioners observe a ten month old girl as she uses her developing physical skills to make social contact. She watches older children playing inside a house in the outdoor area and independently pulls herself up to look in through the window – watching at first and then using eye contact and vocalising to make contact and begin to develop relationships.

Places for exploring and investigating
The baby then uses her newly discovered confidence to explore other special places in the nursery environment. She is encouraged by her key person to explore a pop-up tunnel in the outdoor area.

She discovers the practitioner's sunglasses lying on the ground beside the tunnel and uses gestures and facial expressions to express her interest and 'ask' questions about the sunglasses.

She maintains eye contact with her key person, smiling as she sets off confidently through the tunnel to return the sunglasses to their receptive owner.

Places for communicating

The outdoor environment can be enhanced by the provision of spaces where children can develop their communication skills through interaction with others. Practitioners in the nursery have set up pop-up tents where children can enjoy conversations, share thoughts and ideas and have fun in all weathers.

Larger sheltered spaces for rest and communication are easily created by the children and practitioners using the natural features of the outdoor environment with drapes, ropes and pegs. Building and using these spaces provides many opportunities for groups of children and adults to agree the rules and boundaries for their use.

Places for having privacy
More permanent structures in the outdoor area of a nursery provide spaces where children know their privacy is respected. In the outdoor area of a nursery, a wooden play house with a fenced veranda is popular with groups of children who want a peaceful, quiet place to build their friendships.

Free access to a special place where groups of children can meet in privacy requires a rigorous process of risk assessment and supervision on the part of practitioners, but provides the perfect opportunity for children to develop autonomy and a sense of responsibility towards themselves and others.

Private spaces do not need to be enclosed. A section of the climbing frame is used by a three year old as a special place where she can draw in privacy. Her need for privacy is respected by both practitioners and children.

Places for being creative

An outdoor environment has been carefully set up to allow children to be comfortable out of doors at different times of the year. This will enable them to develop their creativity as they concentrate on outdoor activities which support their interests and fascinations. Practitioners in the nursery make sure children are warm, comfortable and dry by providing the right outerwear and environment.

Places for making choices

Being outside provides a completely different set of opportunities for children to make choices – who they work and play with, what they do, how long they spend on their interests, as well as what and where to eat!

Other things to try

- Make available a range of fabrics, pegs and clips and lengths of wood for the children to make their own special places.

- Use an old fashioned wooden clothes drier to make the frame for a den. Try covering it with camouflage material.

- 'Grow' your own special places using willow structures.

- Make sure that babies and toddlers have small special places to explore – try hanging lightweight fabrics from trees or bushes to create small spaces.

Being 'safety spies'

In the EYFS

The following statements are taken from the Learning and Development requirements of the EYFS, Personal, Social and Emotional Development (Managing feelings and behaviour).

- Children can talk about their own and others' behaviour, and its consequences, and know that some behaviours are unacceptable.

- Children can work as part of a group or class, and understand and follow the rules.

- Children can listen to each other's suggestions and plan how to achieve an outcome without adult help.

Starting points

In a large day nursery for children aged 0–5 the practitioners decide to involve the four year olds in the daily risk assessment of the nursery's outdoor environment. There is much discussion about the challenges and problems faced by the nursery community in making sure that the children of all ages can play safely in the outdoor area.

One of the children suggests that what the nursery needs is a number of 'spies' who can make sure that everywhere is safe to play. The idea of having 'safety spies' is raised by a group of boys who are particularly interested in superhero play.

Learning and development

Building on the children's interest and good ideas for being actively involved in the health and safety of the nursery, the practitioners talk to the children about what they think are the issues that need to be tackled most urgently in the outdoor area. The children come up with four areas of concern:

- Poo (animal droppings)
- Rubbish
- Broken things
- Gates left open

They talk about what equipment they will need to enable them to act as 'safety spies' and collectively, with the help of the practitioner, the group comes up with a recording chart which can be used to check the outdoor area twice a day – at the beginning of both the morning and the afternoon sessions.

On the chart the four areas to be checked are illustrated pictorially with a column for the morning check and one for the afternoon – a ✓ to be added if the area is deemed safe and an ✗ if action is needed. When the action is complete a ✓ is added on top of the ✗.

The children also think that the 'safety spies' need a uniform and they suggest bright fluorescent jackets with 'Safety spy' written on them. The nursery manager makes arrangements to provide the jackets.

Next on the list are an official looking clipboard and pen which the children feel are essential for working outside.

The first check carried out is to discover whether or not there have been any unwelcome guests (animals) in the outdoor area. The spies know the agreed procedures for informing an adult if they discover any animal droppings.

The children work in pairs and often assign each other specific roles. If litter is found in the garden a cross is added to the recording sheet and only when it has been disposed of is the tick of approval given.

Checks are then carried out for any signs of broken or damaged equipment which might prove a hazard. The children take this task very seriously and take into account any problems which could arise for the babies, toddlers and pre-schoolers in the nursery.

Finally, all gates are checked to ensure that the children are secure in the outdoor area. This is often an additoinal opportunity to check for litter or other hazards in the fenced off areas.

When the 'safety spies' have completed their safety audit they report back to the responsible practitioner who acts upon their recommendations.

The check list, safety spy jackets and the clipboards and pens are returned to their place indoors ready for the next safety check to take place.

The children take their responsibility for staying safe very seriously. One of the 'safety spies' raised concerns that the younger children are not always careful when crossing the busy road outside the nursery at the end of the day. With the help of the practitioners, they organise road safety sessions where they show the younger children how to cross the road safely.

The younger children are very attentive to what the four year olds have to say and follow their instructions carefully.

Other things to try

- Make safety signs to place around your setting.
- Invite road safety officers or the fire brigade into your setting to talk about keeping safe.
- Involve the children in planning fire drills or dealing with other emergency situations.
- Talk about different ways of keeping safe when crossing roads on dark evenings.

In the dark

In the EYFS

The following statements are taken from the Learning and Development requirements of the EYFS, Personal, Social and Emotional Development (Self-confidence and self-awareness).

- Children are confident to try new activities and can say why they like some more than others.
- They begin to recognise danger and know who to turn to for help.
- Children are confident to talk to other children when playing together.
- They can say when they do or don't need help.

Starting points

In a large day nursery, practitioners take advantage of the long opening hours of 7.30am to 6.30pm to build up children's confidence and self-awareness by exploring the outdoor area in the dark.

They believe in the suggestion made by Marion Dowling (Personal communication, Hampshire, 2009) that young children enjoy, and benefit from, the well supported experience of 'gratuitous fear'. Being outside in the dark can be a serious challenge for some children but their self-confidence will grow if they are given encouragement by their key person. Before going outside in the dark, the practitioners give the children the experience of a dark den indoors and introduce them to a range of different torches.

Learning and development

A group of toddlers enjoy the experience of being outside in the late afternoon as it's becoming dark. They happily spend time in the garden collecting and sorting leaves and twigs which they have found.

The toddlers appear to be very confident when exploring in the dark, although one of the girls prefers to remain near a practitioner who gives her the responsibility for gathering together the found treasures in a collecting bag, while the rest of the group venture further into the garden to look for natural materials.

An older group of three year olds have very mixed feelings about being outside in the dark. Some are very confident and suggest that they could explore the whole garden if they had torches – which the practitioners provide!

Other children are somewhat more hesitant and one or two children are very apprehensive, insisting on taking comforters out into the garden with them.

The practitioners working with the group are sensitive to the children's feelings, particularly their fears about being in the dark. They encourage the children to talk about their fears and they support them in gaining confidence as they explore the outdoor area.

By supporting each other as they explore, the children become more adventurous. They shine their torches on to the wall creating interesting light effects and shadows.

Some children become very brave venturing into the trees and bushes unaccompanied.

This encourages other members of the group to have the confidence to move away from the practitioners and to explore the darker areas with a friend.

The practitioners support those children who need encouragement to cope with the challenges they face in the dark, giving them the confidence to explore independently, knowing that a sensitive adult is at hand.

The practitioners record the achievements of the individual children as they become more confident, and gain better self-awareness, through their experience of exploring outside in the dark.

Other things to try

- Take the children on a 'light walk' in the local environment to see how many different types of outdoor lights you can find.

- Use your outdoor security light to encourage the children to investigate what happens when they stand in different places.

- Use lights in the outdoor environment at different times of the year to celebrate festivals such as Christmas and Divali.

- Ask the children's parents and carers to help them experience being out in the dark or in moonlight.

Further afield – all year round

In the EYFS

The following statements are taken from the Learning and Development requirements of the EYFS, Personal, Social and Emotional Development (Making relationships).

- Children can play co-operatively, taking turns when playing.

- They resolve minor disagreements through listening to each other to come up with a fair solution.

- Children are confident to speak in a familiar group and will talk about their ideas.

- They can talk about their own and others' behaviour and its consequences.

Starting points

This nursery is committed to ensuring that children enjoy learning out of doors at all times of year, whatever the weather. Practitioners are enthusiastic outdoor explorers themselves and make the most of outdoor learning to provide challenging experiences for children to enjoy.

The nursery has access to a woodland area, where it provides regular Forest School experiences for the three and four year olds, in addition to its well used garden area. The children's adventurous approach to playing and working outside is fostered by practitioners throughout the different seasons of the year.

Learning and development

Outdoors in spring

The children who enjoy the Forest School experience are involved from the outset in agreeing with the practitioners the rules and boundaries which will enable them to enjoy the challenging outdoor area. There is much discussion between adults and children about how they will behave to ensure that the woodland environment is respected.

Having a shared understanding of boundaries and limits means that children are able to challenge themselves both physically and mentally as they solve problems which challenge them.

They are able to develop their confidence safe in the knowledge that competent adults are close at hand should they need help.

The children eagerly work together as a team, testing their relationships, their physical capabilities and their willingness to enjoy risk and challenge.

Outdoors in summer

As the seasons change, the woodland area offers the children different learning opportuntites. The changes in the natural environment present new possibilities for experiences and challenges which interest and excite the children.

Those children who are fascinated by the living things in the woodland are able to focus on their interests during the time spent outdoors. The woodland provides a vast range of living things for the children to discover and investigate.

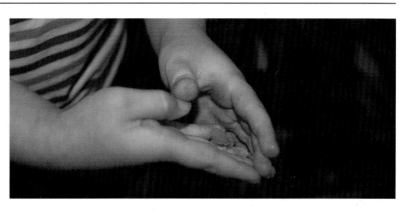

Other children, both girls and boys, are interested in using the available space and materials to create large scale structures.

Two of the girls are working together to build a bridge from fallen branches. They test their physical strength and abilities as they move the branches in a way which remains safe. The task which they have set themselves requires a high degree of co-operation and collaboration.

The girls are observed by two boys who are eager to join the activity. As the children are accustomed to negotiating with each other, the boys are careful to make sure that the girls are happy for them to join in the building project.

When the girls have considered the boys' request they agree that the boys can join their building team. The children spend the rest of the session working together on their building challenge.

The children are able to negotiate, to listen to each other and to display a high level of involvement in their play, building on the previous experiences the practitoners have provided in the nursery.

Outdoors in the autumn

In the autumn the nursery makes changes to its outdoor environment to ensure that the children can continue to set themselves challenges. Large tyres are placed in the nursery grounds for the autumn and winter to support physical play.

When the new equipment is introduced to the outdoor area, the children and practitioners spend time agreeing rules about how it is used, ensuring that all of the children can play safely and securely.

Outdoors in winter

As the weather changes and early morning frosts arrive, the children enjoy exploring the outdoor area with all their senses. They test their ideas and theories about frost and ice, freezing and melting and share these thoughts with their friends.

Despite the cold weather the children show high levels of involvement in the activities which interest them.

As they follow their personal interests the children spend long periods of time absorbed in their investigations, despite the cold weather.

Practitioners in the nursery believe that being outside in all weathers provides many special opportunities for children to be interested, excited and motivated to learn.

Other things to try

Take the children for a special walk for each season.

- Spring walk – look for signs of spring such as new leaves and buds, flowers, birds nesting, spring fashions in shops, garden centre and DIY stores spring offers.

- Summer walk – look for shadows in the environment; those that move, those that stay still, dark shadows and pale shadows. Go on a 'smell safari' around the local area.

- Autumn walk – look for signs of autumn in both the natural and the built environments, in parks, hedgerows, gardens, shops and markets.

- Winter walk – look carefully for all the different ways we use ICT to keep people and traffic safe in cold, dull weather – traffic lights, street lights, car headlights and fog lights, pedestrian controlled lights.

❝Having a shared understanding of boundaries and limits means that children are able to challenge themselves both physically and mentally as they solve problems which challenge them.❞

An environment for Physical Development

In the EYFS

The following statements are taken from the Learning and Development requirements of the EYFS, Physical Development.

Provide opportunities for young children to:

- Be active and interactive.

- Develop their co-ordination, control and movement.

Help children to:

- Understand the importance of physical activity.

- Talk about ways to keep healthy and safe.

Starting points

The pedagogical approach in Reggio Emilia is founded on the image of children as competent, confident and rich in potential. Educators encourage children to take calculated risks within a safe environment, both indoors and out of doors.

The EYFS requires practitioners to view children as competent, confident individuals, respecting their efforts when facing challenges, encouraging them to be independent as they make choices and try things out.

Nurseries and home-based carers can provide opportunities for young children to experience risk and challenge within a safe environment in their outdoor area, at the local park or further afield on visits and regular Forest School programmes.

Learning and development

In the park

For home-based carers and early years settings which do not have a large outdoor area, the local park can provide an excellent outdoor environment for supporting children's physical development.

Young children have a biological drive to use their bodies and develop their physical skills. A home-based carer visits the local park on a daily basis and encourages the children to become independent as they negotiate the large equipment in the playground.

A one year old girl is excited by her own developing mobility skills and sets herself physical challenges as she plays. The practitoner allows plenty of time for the toddler to practise her skills, praising and supporting her as she negotiates the slide.

A two year old becomes preoccupied with moving the outdoor chess pieces away from the large chequered board in the park. She works tirelessly, pushing her physical skills and capabilities to their limits as she lifts and carries the resin chess pieces.

After ten minutes she has cleared the outdoor chess board providing herself with a clear, safe area for running and dancing. The girl's carer is quietly attentive while the chess pieces are being moved, encouraging the toddler to enjoy her risky freedom.

Older children use the large play equipment in the local park to develop their physical skills of climbing, balancing and sliding. They understand the need for safety and learn to respect other children's personal space when playing as a group.

In the nursery grounds

After one of the children in a nursery sees a film at home about an army assault course he tells his friends and the practitioners at his nursery all about it. The children decide that they want to create an obstacle course using the play equipment which is spread out across the outdoor area of the nursery.

The practitioners help the children to move the equipment into their suggested order for the assault course. They observe the children as they use the equipment, allowing them the time and space to enjoy their risky freedom in a safe and secure environment.

The practitioners take note of which children are confident in taking manageable risks in their play.

They notice which children are able to balance as they negotiate the equipment...

... and the different ways the children find of moving across and on and off objects.

The obstacle course planned by the children provides many opportunities for them to experiment with different ways of moving, to manage themselves safely and to show that they can move with confidence and imagination.

Forest School visits
Further afield in the outdoors, a school-based nursery uses an area of forest land to provide a challenging physical environment for the children through a regular Forest School programme. The children have opportunities to climb up slopes which can be rough or slippery, requiring careful physical movements.

They are then encouraged to slide and slither back down the slope, taking turns and showing an understanding of the need for safety as they tackle this new challenge.

Taking part in Forest School activities helps the children learn how to manage risk and challenge safely. They learn about physical boundaries and accepting rules as they collaborate in the task of toasting marshmallows on an open fire.

The regular Forest School visits provide some of the most challenging, and exciting, outdoor environments for physical development experienced by children in the early years. However, all early years practitioners can ensure that all children have opportunities, time and space to enjoy energetic play on a daily basis by using their own outdoor area or the local park.

Other things to try

- Set challenges for toddlers which involve crawling, climbing, walking, throwing and catching.

- Use blocks and planks to create a balancing challenge for older children.

- Mark out boundaries for ball games or for using the wheeled toys to ensure that children can play safely.

- Use outdoor play opportunities to encourage the children to use movement vocabulary such as 'follow', 'lead', 'start', 'stop', 'quickly' and 'slowly'.

Active babies and toddlers

In the EYFS

The following statements are taken from the Learning and Development requirements of the EYFS, Physical Development (Moving and handling).

- Children gain increasing control of their whole bodies.

- They show good control and co-ordination in large and small movements.

- Children become aware of how to negotiate the space and objects around them.

- They negotiate space successfully when playing... adjusting speed or changing direction to avoid obstacles.

Starting points

In a day nursery the practitioners place great value on ensuring that all children have access to the outdoor environment on a daily basis.

As in many nurseries it's not always easy to make this happen, particularly if the rooms for the babies and toddlers are up a flight of stairs. The practitioners include the development of stair climbing skills as part of their planning for the children's physical development. They ensure that the youngest children are outside on a daily basis whatever the weather – by going for walks, playing in the garden and by enjoying everyday activities out of doors whenever possible.

Learning and development

Instead of providing only traditional toys for the babies to play with outside, the practitioners from the baby room set up a range of interesting exploration trays. The babies enjoy playing with the kitchen utensils and other metal objects in a tray of water. The practitioners observe which items the babies reach for and how they develop their skills of grasping, squeezing and picking things up. They take note of what each of the babies chooses to do with their chosen resource and use their observations to provide new activities to develop the children's physical skills.

The older babies begin to extend their physical capabilities, including their coordination skills, by using rocking toys which are the right size to enable the children to access them independently.

Nursery staff provide a variety of tunnels in the outdoor area to stimulate and challenge the babies and toddlers. The transparent tunnels provide an exciting, but secure, environment for the children to creep and crawl through.

The babies and toddlers develop their physical skills as they vary the pace at which they travel through the tunnels.

From a very early age the children are interested in wheels and how things move. The nursery staff provide a wide range of wheeled toys suitable for different ages of children. The babies enjoy pushing and pulling small wheeled toys and trying them out on different surfaces.

The older toddlers are often interested in the wheels themselves and how they move. As they explore the mechanics and the patterns of movement of the wheeled toys, they use language to describe how things move when they are turned, pushed or pulled.

Some of the children set themselves challenges involving the large tyres in the outdoor area, using their developing strength and skills to lift, balance and roll the tyres.

Others enlist the help of the practitioners to create a stack of tyres for climbing up and jumping off. By building their own climbing equipment using the tyres the children have control over how they play, pushing themselves to the limit of their physical capabilities.

Other things to try

- Encourage the children to experience a wide range of surfaces as they play, helping them to understand how to move safely in different places.

- Make outdoor collections of natural materials and provide suitable containers for the children to enjoy heuristic play out of doors.

- Hang resources that move or make a noise from bushes or branches to encourage babies and toddlers to reach and touch them.

- Provide a collection of different types of balls so that the babies and toddlers can observe how they roll and bounce and how they behave when thrown.

Developing physical skills

In the EYFS

The following statements are taken from the Learning and Development requirements of the EYFS, Physical Development (Moving and handling).

- Children must be helped to understand the importance of physical activity.
- Provide opportunities for young children to be active... and to develop their co-ordination, control and movement.
- Children move confidently in a range of ways, safely negotiating space.

Starting points

In a wide range of early years settings the role of early years practitioners working with children of all ages is to promote awareness of a healthy lifestyle. This involves practitioners ensuring that children learn from an early age that exercise has a positive effect on their bodies and their health.

The practitioners ensure that they provide children with interesting equipment so that they are motivated to enjoy outside exercise daily – come rain or shine!

Learning and development

A sixteen month old girl visits the local park with her carer several times a week. She has well-developed physical skills and enjoys new physical challenges. As the toddler regularly plays enthusiastically with a large ball in the park, her carer decides to see what happens when she introduces a different shaped ball.

The toddler looks closely at the ball, recognising that it is different from the other balls she is more familiar with, before holding it at arm's length and letting it drop.

The way the ball bounces fascinates the toddler and she repeats the action several times, observing the ways in which the ball falls and bounces. She is amused by what happens when she kicks the ball. She continues to practise her skills for a sustained period of time.

At different times of the year the practitioners at a day nursery introduce a variety of large and small physical play equipment so that outdoor play is varied and does not become repetitive. They are careful to ensure that there is sufficient equipment available for the children to avoid squabbles and long periods of inactivity.

In the summer months equipment is introduced into the outdoor area to give the children opportunities to move in different ways and at different speeds. When the three year olds are ready for a new challenge the practitioners introduce 'animal sacks' to enable them to develop their jumping and balance skills.

In colder weather, outdoor play is enhanced by the addition of novel equipment which interests the children and encourages them to use it. In the nursery the practitioners have provided equipment which can be used either to jump over or to 'limbo dance' underneath.

The simple set of limbo equipment creates a lot of interest amongst the children and they soon set up competitions to see who can perform the best. The activity requires the children to move with increasing control and co-ordination, creating a physical challenge which gives them an opportunity to refine and improve their actions.

Throughout the year the practitioners organise lively games which encourage the children to be active and energetic. Simple running activities are held all year round, providing the grass surface is safe and not too slippery.

Other things to try

- Provide large boxes for children to crawl through and ladders to climb on.
- Provide a selection of balls which behave differently for the youngest children to use out of doors.
- Organise a mini Olympics to practise movement skills using beanbags, cones, balls and hoops.
- Have fun with an egg and spoon race using hardboiled eggs and serving spoons or racquets and soft balls.

Further afield - the mammoth trap

In the EYFS

The following statements are taken from the Learning and Development requirements of the EYFS, Physical Development (Moving and handling, Health and self-care).

- Children show good control and co-ordination in large and small movements.

- They move confidently in a range of ways, safely negotiating space.

- They handle tools effectively.

Starting points

A day nursery organises Forest School experiences for the three and four years olds in the pre-school section to extend its outdoor provision. Groups of children visit a local woodland area on a weekly basis throughout the year in all weathers.

The children and practitioners build their knowledge and experience throughout the nursery year which begins in September. Each group of children has its favourite routes through the woodland, special places to go and things to do.

Learning and development

On the journey to the woodland, on a crisp December day, one of the groups of four year olds discusses what they would like to do in the wood when they arrive.

Building on an interest in dinosaurs which they have been investigating in the nursery, one of the children suggests that there must be dinosaurs living in the wood. The group agree that it is likely that pre-historic creatures live there and come up with the idea of building a trap to catch a mammoth. The children and adults agree that this is what they will focus on during the morning.

One of the boys suggests that the best place to trap the mammoth would be in the 'big ditch' in the middle of the wood and the group sets off along a route which they know well. En route to the ditch the children stop off at the special places which they visit every week. The first stop is the 'little jumping tree'...

... closely followed by the 'big jumping tree', both of which are aptly named as places where the children practise jumping off the trees and landing safely. They then progress through the woodland until they come to the place where the rusty oil drums can be found.

The practitioners have carried out a risk/benefit analysis of all of the aspects of the woodland, including the old oil drums, and have concluded that the benefits of exploring the drums outweigh the risks posed to the children. The children respect the agreed rules and boundaries when playing in the woodland, and derive great pleasure from the challenges posed by trying to move the drums safely.

The same rules apply at the next stopping point where the children enjoy dropping and breaking the large pieces of chalk which are to be found naturally in the wood.

Eventually they arrive at the 'big ditch' and begin to build their mammoth trap. One group of children collect long branches which are to be found near the ditch and begin the task of covering the hole.

This is a time consuming process and the children work tirelessly as a team for forty minutes creating a mat of branches across the ditch. They cooperate in lifting, carrying and arranging the unwieldy branches. As they work they talk about what they are doing and how excited they are feeling at the thought of catching a mammoth.

Meanwhile, another group of children spends time hammering pointy sticks at the side of the ditch with the intention of tripping the mammoth and making it fall into the trap. One of the girls becomes concerned about whether or not the mammoth could hurt his knees on the sticks as they want to capture the mammoth, not harm it.

Finally the mammoth trap is completed to the children's satisfaction...

... and they retreat further into the woods to wait to see whether or not a mammoth will be caught in their trap.

Soon the waiting becomes too much and one of the boys is nominated to check whether or not the trap has been successful. He makes his way slowly and carefully down the slope to the mammoth trap.

Sadly there is no mammoth to be found in the trap so the children decide to play in it themselves before removing the large branches to leave the area of woodland safe.

They leave two thick branches over the ditch to use as a bridge and they catch, not a mammoth, but an enthusiastic practitioner! The children all agree that they have had a very successful morning at Forest School.

Other things to try

- Whilst keeping safety as a paramount concern, consider using a risk/benefit analysis when planning outdoor experiences for the children.

- Involve the children in devising rules to ensure safety in aspects of outdoor play.

- Teach the children the skills of using tools and materials and provide many opportunities for them to practise their skills.

- Provide logs, branches, barrels and other large scale open-ended objects for children to use in their outdoor play.

An environment for Communication and Language, Literacy

In the EYFS

The following statements are taken from the Learning and Development requirements of the EYFS, Communication and Language, and Literacy.

- Give children opportunities to:
  - Speak and listen in a range of situations.
  - Develop their confidence and skills in expressing themselves.

- Encourage children to read and write, both through listening to others reading, and being encouraged to begin to read and write themselves.

- Give children a wide range of reading materials – books, poems and other written materials, to ignite their interest.

Starting points

In the Reggio Approach to early childhood a wise use of time is valued for all the different opportunities it provides. In their daily life the children are entitled to have time to be, to do, to meet, to play, to think and reflect, to talk, to listen, to rest and to eat. The learning environment is planned so that children can spend long periods of uninterrupted time on developing their interests, fascinations and communication skills.

Many nurseries in the UK have developed their use of the outdoor environment to ensure that children can take advantage of the many opportunities to talk, listen, enjoy books and mark make which being out of doors presents.

Learning and development

Mark making
In one nursery the practitioners have thought very carefully about how best to provide interesting mark making materials and outdoor 'furnishings' at a suitable height for the children to use. They have provided recycled cable rolls to use as mark making surfaces that are just the right height for the 18-36 month olds.

Having made available large chalks and water for the children to explore, the adults join the mark making activity modelling what happens when the chalks mixed with water are manipulated on the surface of the 'table'.

Soon a conversation develops about colour mixing and the children follow the lead given by the practitioner, mark making with the chalks and with their hands.

Enjoying books

The youngest children in a nursery enjoy a regular visit to the local library to join in with storytelling sessions and to start to develop an appreciation of books. Whilst the children are initially attracted to the appealing book storage, they very soon become engaged by the selection of books on offer.

The practitioners encourage the children to browse through the books before making their selection to take back to the nursery. A regular walk to the library not only provides the children with an experience which they might not normally have, but also introduces them to their local environment. There are many opportunities for the practitioners and the children to talk about what they can see on their journey.

Back in the nursery, suitable ground covers and waterproof cushions and beanbags are readily available for children to create their own outdoor spaces. Here they can share books with their friends, without the need for an adult to be present.

Speaking and listening

In a nursery class with access to a small area of woodland, the children and adults have created a sheltered area for storytelling using a large tarpaulin as a roof and logs for seating. This sheltered area is used all year round and in all weathers.

Another favourite place in the wood for telling stories and having conversations is among the roots of the fallen 'Storytelling tree.' The possibilities suggested by the magic of the woodland leads to wonderful stories being told which are packed full of adventure and fantasy.

Other things to try

- Encourage collaborative mark making on a large scale out of doors. Provide large blackboards, use paths and walls, or hang large sheets of paper on a fence or tree.

- Make sure that there are seats, cushions, mats, clipboards and other suitable surfaces available in the outdoor area to encourage reading and mark making.

- With the children, make a collection of mark making materials using natural resources found in your garden or in the local environment.

- Create a special storytelling space in your outdoor area which can be used by adults and children together or independently by the children.

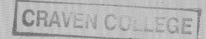

Sun catchers

> ## In the EYFS
>
> The following statements are taken from the Learning and Development requirements of the EYFS, Communication and Language (Understanding and Speaking).
>
> - Children answer 'how' and 'why' questions about their experiences and in response to ...events.
> - Children develop their own narratives and explanations by connecting ideas or events.
> - Children show some awareness of the listener by making changes to language and non-verbal features.
> - They recount experiences and imagine possibilities, often connecting ideas.

Starting points

In the pre-school room of a large day nursery the children are interested in making a 'weather box' for the garden. They plan to make various items that will help them to explore different types of weather. The children talk about how they could create windmills, wind chimes and kites and then the idea of catching the sun arises.

Practitioners in the nursery are experienced in documenting children's learning which they see as a vital step in observing children's interests and fascinations in order to plan experiences that will engage children and extend their learning and development. They record the actual words that the children say in order to better understand what they are thinking.

The practitioners and children pose questions and suggest possible answers, often based on the children's prior knowledge.

Where's the sun? *"Outside" says one of the boys. "Hiding in the trees and the bushes." "Maybe it's under one of these!" a second boy lifts up a lid from the table. "It's all around, it moves everywhere" offers one of the girls.*

The children set off to find the sun in the outdoor area.

Learning and development

Once outside the children carry on the process of working out how they can solve the challenge they have set themselves.

How can we catch the sun? *"In a measuring box" suggests one of the girls. "You need to catch the sun then you can measure the sun. You need a big long stick to catch the long sun" says a boy. "What if we paint something blue and the sun would come down and the sun would think that it's a piece of the sky that's come down" is another suggestion from a second girl. "It could just go down like it's going to bed like at night when the moon comes out."*

Many more ideas come from the children and they listen carefully to each other's suggestions, politely pointing out where theories might not work.

"You need a net like when you catch butterflies." "Maybe have a long long long long long rod then we put the sun into a bottle." "That wouldn't work cuz the bottle would break. The sun is big and round. It would break the bottle."

Some of the boys have a very practical approach to solving the problem.

"A bucket and when the sun comes out of the cloud and it's wobbling, it'll fall into the bucket." "You could grab the sun with your hands." "We can't touch it coz it will make us on fire" "We need gloves on. You need gloves on to catch the sun with your hands."

The children decide that they should try to create sun catchers themselves. They look through the materials available to them in their creative studio area indoors.

They look at materials which they think might attract the sun – transparent, translucent and reflective materials which the children feel have properties that might catch the sun.

As they test the materials and consider how they might be used, the children talk about the sort of features their sun catchers will need – long poles and attractive materials.

They discuss their ideas with each other, explain to each other what they are doing and talk about what they think they will need to do next.

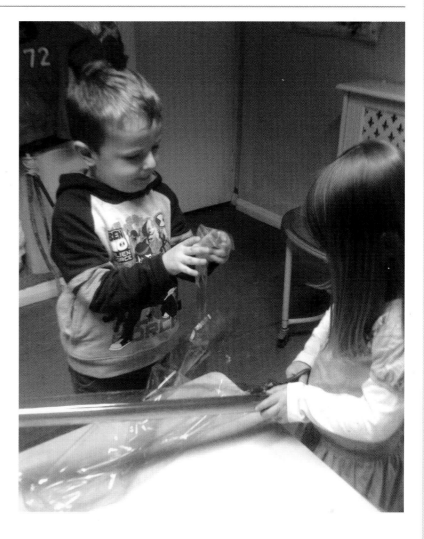

Groups of children work together collaboratively to make their large scale sun catchers. They elaborate on their ideas and use a widening vocabulary as they communicate with, and learn from, each other.

When the sun catchers are complete the children take them out into the outdoor area to test them. Some of the children have created hand-held sun catchers which they test in small groups, explaining what they are doing to the younger children and practitioners in the garden.

Others have designed, and made, sun catchers which need to placed higher up in the trees. With the help of the practitioners they place them in the branches of different trees, hoping to see which of them catches the sun first.

Throughout the day the children observe the sun catchers and become involved in discussions about whether or not they are in the right position, if they are the right shape and whether they could have been designed differently.

Eventually the children notice that the sun catchers are shining as they catch the light in the sunshine and they decide that their designs may not have done exactly what they thought they would do but they have certainly 'caught the sun!'

Other things to try

Encourage the children to think, talk about, and investigate other 'big questions' which interest them, such as:

- **How can you trap your shadow?**
- **Can you catch the wind?**
- **How do birds fly?**
- **Can you blow a square bubble?**

Making marks with a feather

In the EYFS

The following statements are taken from the Learning and Development requirements of the EYFS, Communication and Language (Writing) in addition to Physical Development (Moving and Handling).

- Children give meaning to marks they make as they draw, write and paint.
- They can segment words orally.
- Children use some clearly identifiable letters to communicate meaning.
- They hold their paper in position and use their preferred hand for writing, using a correct pencil grip.

Starting points

In a day nursery the practitioners introduce a stuffed bird into the outdoor environment as a provocation to the children – to provoke their thoughts, ideas and suggestions for activities which interest them.

The bird is simply left on the picnic table outside and the practitioners wait to see what they children do and say.

Several of the three and four year olds are intrigued by the bird, particularly by its beak, feet and feathers.

Learning and development

An interesting conversation develops when one of the three year olds finds a feather in the garden. A four year old boy draws on his previous knowledge and tells the group of children that feathers used to be used to write with in the olden days.

The practitioners talk to the children about writing with quills and ink and they agree to the children's suggestion that they would like to try to write with feathers.

A feather hunt ensues in the outdoor area and a range of different sized feathers are found. Other feathers are brought outside from the studio area by the children and the practitioners provide bottles of ink and paper.

The children become engrossed in making marks with feathers and ink, concentrating intently and for extended periods of time.

The three year olds experiment with a variety of feathers, controlling the feathers with confidence and making a range of different marks on their paper.

The four year olds make even more precise marks as they experiment with the feathers.

The practitioners place a variety of mark making tools on the outdoor table where the children are working and wait to see what happens.

The three year olds move on from using the feathers for their mark making to using brushes and pens with nibs with the ink.

The group of children continue to develop their writing skills in a very calm and quiet manner.

The children continue to select different mark making tools as they experiment with their writing. The practitioners observe how the children handle and manipulate the writing implements and the level of control which they demonstrate as they write.

The older children are equally intrigued by the mark making activity and they work for sustained periods of time on making marks and writing letters and simple words.

The practitioners have provided a provocation which leads to an activity that fascinates the children and allows them to develop their own ideas and interests whilst providing a perfect opportunity for them to experiment with writing.

Other things to try

- Make sure that clip boards are provided for children to use when writing outside.
- Help the children to make their own scrapbooks, using a variety of different papers, for drawing and writing outdoors.
- Provide other implements such as twigs, pea sticks and dried stems to write with.
- When the weather permits, set up a writing area outside so that mark making becomes an integral part of children's play.

Further afield – letters and words

In the EYFS

The following statements are taken from the Learning and Development requirements of the EYFS, Literacy (Reading and Writing).

- Children know that print carries meaning.

- They give meaning to marks they make as they draw, write and paint.

- Children can segment words orally, and use some clearly identifiable letters to communicate meaning, representing some sounds correctly and in sequence.

- They use their phonic knowledge to spell words in ways which match their spoken sounds.

Starting points

In the pre-school section of a nursery the practitioners create an environment which is rich in print, by using traditional names and labels and by valuing a range of presentational techniques when documenting the children's learning.

Opportunities are taken in the outdoor area to create examples of environmental print which are relevant to the children's lives – and at their physical level. The nursery minibus has its own bus stop with a sign which can be understood by children of all ages in the nursery.

Learning and development

The pre-school children are interested in signs and symbols and talk about the different examples they see on their way to nursery and when they are out and about with their families. They decide to investigate the different environmental print they can find in the local area.

The practitioners talk to the children about how best they can spot signs and symbols in the town where they live. As they are about to go on a visit to a garden centre to buy plants for the garden, the children decide to incorporate a sign spotting activity in their journey.

Before they set off, the pre-schoolers 'spot' signs outside the nursery, including the symbols and words on the minibus. They have paper and pencils to record the environmental print that they see.

The journey is delayed a little as the children discuss, with the practitioners, what the words on the side of the minibus mean. They think that the imagery on the minibus reminds them of a journey which in turn reminds them that they are on their way to the garden centre.

a hundred ways to care
a hundred worlds to invent

While they are travelling on the minibus the children play 'I-Spy' signs, symbols, letters and words.

At the garden centre the hunt for signs continues and discussions are held about what the signs say and what they mean. Some of the children are keen to point out numbers, letters and words which they recognise and can name.

Back in the nursery in the afternoon, the practitioners decide to capitalise on the children's interest in letters by organising a letter hunt in the garden.

At lunchtime one of the practitioners hides the lower case letters of the alphabet for the children to find. They set off with great enthusiasm to search for the lower case letters.

With the help of the practitioners the children secure the letters they have found to the outdoor blackboard in alphabetical order.

They enjoy reciting the letters in alphabetical order, recognising and identifying the letters in turn.

The practitioners develop the children's interest by placing a flip chart and pens next to the blackboard area for the children to use. The children begin to select letters which are meaningful to them, such as the first letters in their names or family members (Zoë, daddy, mummy). They use the letters to help them sound out the initial sounds and to spell familiar names and words.

Some of the children continue to write words they know without using the letters as prompts. They use their phonic knowledge to write simple regular words and to make good attempts at more complex words. These skills are warmly praised by their peers.

The following day the practitioners make available a new set of resources which will encourage the children to develop their interest in letters. This time they provide stencils of both upper and lower case letters which they children decide to use alongside the blackboard, brushes and water – and a whole new writing journey begins.

Other things to try

- Take photographs of signs and environmental print in your local neighbourhood. Play games where the children recognise what the signs say.

- Make signs for the outdoor environment so that people can find their way around, move and play safely, know where things are kept, and how to look after the environment.

- Turn the wheeled toys into different vehicles using cardboard boxes. Design signs and slogans for the vehicles.

- Encourage the children to look at different ways of improving the outdoor environment by introducing planters, litter bins and recycling points with their own signs.

An environment for Mathematics

In the EYFS

The following statements are taken from the Learning and Development requirements of the EYFS, Mathematics.

Provide opportunities for children to:

- Practise and improve their skills in counting.
- Calculate simple addition and subtraction problems.
- Describe shapes, spaces and measures.

Starting points

Provision for children's learning in Mathematics is, like the other areas of learning, closely connected with their developing ability to be creative and think critically.

Creativity is fundamental to the Reggio Approach to early childhood. Nurseries in the UK who take their inspiration from the approach think about how they can:

- develop 'creative spaces, indoors and outside
- provide open-ended resources for the children to use
- listen to the many different ways in which children express themselves.

This helps children develop their own ideas, make links between ideas and develop strategies for doing things.

Learning and development

A carefully designed outdoor environment is rich in possibilities for mathematical development. It provides children with opportunities to count objects and also when playing games such as jumping and climbing games, to recognise shapes and to develop an understanding of shapes, measures and distances.

In one nursery there is a covered section of the outdoor area where exploration and problem solving takes place all year round. There are many opportunities for mathematical problem solving on a large scale at the large water tray; these are enhanced by the provision of wide range of containers, tubing and funnels for the children to select and use.

This outdoor space also contains a sunken lidded sand pit which is either used for sand play or is covered to provide a larger decking area for problem solving activities on a large scale.

The covered space includes bricks, wooden blocks and an easel for children to record their mathematical ideas and problem solving.

The wooden stairs leading from inside to the outdoor area are numbered using brass door numbers mirroring the numbers on the indoor staircases. This gives the children opportunities to develop their skills in recognising numerals, counting on and counting back and inventing and playing number games on the steps.

The two and a half and three year olds enjoy free access to the outdoor area where they are often involved in building roads and pathways with the wooden blocks. The practitioners encourage the use of programmable electronic toys, such as the Bee-bot, out of doors to extend the children's thinking skills as they develop their understanding of maths to solve mathematical problems which arise as they play.

When the children show a particular interest in aspects of mathematical understanding, the practitioners create discrete areas for them to explore their developing ideas. A builder's tray is filled with mixed pulses for the children to investigate using sieves, funnels and a variety of spoons and containers. The activity is enhanced by the addition of a balance scale and a 'real' set of kitchen scales.

In a Montessori nursery the outdoor area is set up to encourage the children to investigate mathematical challenges independently. The children develop their understanding of numbers and measures from an early age due to the careful organisation of the environment and the resources which are provided.

The containers of water are securely positioned at a height appropriate for the children and a rich variety of pots, bowls and buckets are provided along with waterproof clothing. The practitioners observe the children carefully as they play, in order to provide further opportunities to support the children's interests.

The older children develop their problem solving skills through free access to the resources in the outdoor area. One of the boys decides that he wants to observe and measure the flow of water from a funnel through a tube. He enlists the help of a practitioner and asks her to wedge the funnel in the lower branches of the tree.

There is then much discussion amongst the children as to how they will reach the funnel to pour the water in and where the water will go when it is poured into the funnel. The first problem is solved by the children working out which size of crate they will need, and where it will be positioned, to help them reach the funnel.

The second challenge is solved by the group of children carefully measuring, and positioning, clear tubing for the water to flow through.

Having observed that the water gets 'stuck' at some points in the tubing, the children refine their plan to ensure that the water is flowing on a downward path.

In both nurseries the value of the outdoor environment as a mathematical resource has been recognised, with practitioners paying attention to the equipment which is provided and how it is stored to enable the children to have free access.

Whenever possible the practitioners encourage the children to record what they have done and what they have been thinking. By providing the resources children need to record the methods they use to answer problems they pose out of doors, practitioners can observe, and note, the many different ways in which children express themselves.

Other things to try

- Create a permanent, or semi-permanent, number line along the bricks of a wall.
- Use containers of natural materials – conkers, leaves, stones, shells – for counting and calculating outside.
- Provide a bucket on a pulley so that children can use larger quantities of resources for estimating and measuring 'heavier' and 'lighter'.
- Create a 'maths trail' in your outdoor area or local environment looking for numbers, shapes and measures in the environment.

Out for the count!

In the EYFS

The following statements are taken from the Learning and Development requirements of the EYFS, Mathematics (Numbers, Shape, space and measures).

- Children show curiosity about numbers by offering comments or asking questions.

- They use numbers up to 10 to do simple addition and subtraction to solve practical problems.

- Children can find a total by counting on, and can calculate how many are left from a larger number by counting back.

- Children use everyday language to describe and compare size, position and distance.

Starting points

Many early years practitioners in the UK encourage the children in their care to make good use of natural and reclaimed materials in all areas of their learning and development. The outdoor environment provides both the perfect opportunity for children to explore the natural world and the space to use open ended resources on a large scale.

Learning and development

These two year old girls in a day nursery are interested in the knobbly bumps on the trunks of the trees. The girls are particularly interested in the number '2' which is special to their group of two year old friends. They begin to count the bumps they can find: '1,2-1,2-1,2' pointing to the bumps as they count.

Having watched the girls counting, one of the boys decides to count the 'leaves' on a small conifer, reciting the number names 1 to 6 in order as he touches the tree. He realises that he needs to count beyond 6 and uses the number names 7-10, not always in the correct order.

Some of the other two year olds are investigating what happens when they put different objects into buckets of water. Once again, their interest lies in putting two objects into each bucket, counting '1,2' as they do so.

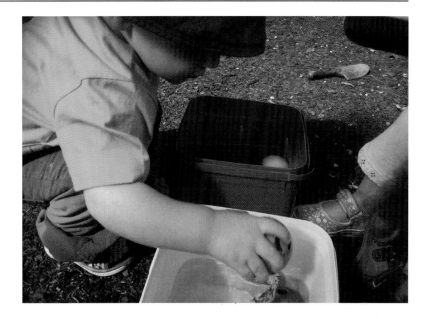

The toddlers talk about putting 'more' things into the buckets. They count '1-2-3' as they add three corks to the water and then add more objects. When the practitioner asks the children how many objects are in the water they explain that they have more than two and more than three without venturing to count further. The practitioner helps the children to count the five objects in the bucket.

In a Montessori nursery the three and four year olds use nursery equipment and reclaimed resources in their play to raise and solve mathematical challenges. Two of the boys are involved in a role play scenario which involves firefighters at work. While protecting a building, they line up the available cones, counting them as they do so. As they add the cones to the line one at a time, they count how many they have left in the box the cones are stored in.

Later in the morning a third firefighter decides to store the cones inside the top of the building. As he picks up the cones one by one he discovers that he has a physical challenge in reaching the top of the large cardboard tube. There is much discussion about things which are 'too high' 'taller' and 'smaller'.

With perseverance, the firefighter puts the cones on to the top of the building one by one, counting how many cones are still in the line and how many have been put into the tube. By providing opportunties for children to count things which interest them out of doors, the practitoners encourage the development of the children's understanding of numbers and their use of mathematical language.

Other things to try

- Provide containers of reclaimed materials such as corks, buttons, cotton reels or bottle tops which can be counted and sorted alongside natural materials outside.

- Enhance role-play out of doors by providing props which can be counted and examples of numerals such as number plates for the wheeled toys.

- Plant rows of flowers or vegetables which can be counted regularly by the children.

- Use the space outside to play number games and sing number songs – have fun with ten green (plastic) bottles sitting on a wall.

" The outdoor environment provides both the perfect opportunity for children to explore the natural world and the space to use open ended resources on a large scale. "

Measuring shadows

In the EYFS

The following statements are taken from the Learning and Development requirements of the EYFS, Mathematics (Shape, space and measures).

- Children can describe their relative position such as 'behind' or 'next to'.

- They can compare properties of objects which are 'big' or 'small'.

- They use everyday language to describe and compare size, position and distance.

- Children estimate, measure, weigh and compare and order objects and talk about properties and position.

Starting points

In a day nursery the children are encouraged, from a very early age, to play with light and shadow at different times of the year. They develop a keen interest in the shapes and sizes of their shadows and how they change over time.

The practitioners are aware that shadows fascinate children of all ages and the outdoor environment is the perfect place to explore them. By carefully documenting children's actions and words the practitioners gain an understanding of how individual children are developing their understanding of shape, space and measures.

Learning and development

The two year olds in the nursery discover their shadows on a sunny autumn day. They are intrigued by their length, position and movement.

They notice that the bikes' shadows are pointing in the same direction as their own and they become engrossed in finding out how they can make the shadows overlap. They begin to use a variety of words to describe the size, shapes and position of the shadows they are exploring.

The practitoners working with the two year olds take note of the children's observations and use the photographs later in the day to remind the children of their mathematical investigations.

During the summer months the pre-school children also become interested in their shadows, in particular they are interested in the positions of their shadows and the length of their shadows compared to themselves.

They talk about which is bigger, smaller, shorter and taller as well as using positional language such as in front of, to the side, to the left and to the right.

Two of the pre-school boys decide that they want to measure their shadows more accurately and spend a lot of time debating how they can do this. After some lengthy discussions with a practitioner, they decide that they could capture their shadows by drawing round them and then measuring them. Once the shadows are drawn around, the boys consider what might be the best way to measure them.

As the children are encouraged to use mathematical resources and equipment both indoors and outside, they consider several solutions to their problem and decide that using unifix cubes would be the best method of measuring the length of the shadows.

The boys solve their measuring problem by linking the cubes together and placing them along the length, and the across the width, of their shadows.

The problem the boys set for themselves involves counting large numbers of unfix cubes and enables them to describe and compare the size of their shadows with a degree of accuracy that they are happy with.

Other things to try

- Go on a shadow hunt in your garden or the local area. Look for big, small, tall, short, narrow and wide shadows.

- On a sunny day, look around the outdoor area for clearly identifiable shadows. Observe how the position of the shadows change during the day and record your investigation by taking photographs.

- Develop the children's interest in shadows by creating a large sundial using a pole in the ground and marking the position of the sun each hour.

- Measure the changes in the size and shape of a puddle in the outdoor area by drawing round the puddle throughout the day as it evaporates and becomes smaller.

"By carefully documenting children's actions and words the practitioners gain an understanding of how individual children are developing their understanding of shape, space and measures."

Further afield – all about clocks

In the EYFS

The following statements are taken from the Learning and Development requirements of the EYFS, Mathematics (Numbers, Shape, space and measures).

- Children show curiosity about numbers by offering comments or asking questions.
- They use numbers up to 10 in order to do simple addition and subtraction to solve practical problems.
- Children can compare properties of objects which are 'big' or 'small.' They can describe their relative position such 'behind' or 'next to'.
- They use everyday language to describe and compare size, weight, capacity, position and distance.

Starting points

Being out of doors provides a rich range of mathematical possibilities, many of which occur spontaneously. The outdoor environment is naturally shaped by the mathematical notion of time – times of the day, patterns of the year and seasonal changes. Practitioners committed to outdoor learning can take advantage of the many opportunities for mathematical development the wider environment provides.

Learning and development

In a day nursery the children are fascinated by the dandelion clocks which they have found growing in the garden, providing a wonderful reason to count and an opportunity to introduce young children to the notion of measuring time.

Their interest in telling the time is picked up by the practitioners who take the opportunity to introduce other systems for telling the time.

A group of girls are particularly interested in a practitioner's watch and they are eager to discover whether or not it ticks like the clocks they have at home.

At lunch time the practitioners collect together resources which they think will interest the children during the afternoon.

One of the girls is intrigued by the large red wall clock – the numerals, the moving pointers and the loud tick the clock makes. She decides to share her findings with a friend who shares her interest.

The girls continue to explore the collection of time related resources in ways which are of interest to them as individuals. They look carefully at the watch faces and the pictures of famous clocks to help them see the different numerals and how the pointers move.

The ticks made by the watch, or lack of them, puzzle the girls as they try to work out the difference between the clock and the watches. They come up with many interesting theories about why the two are different.

Having explored the watches and clocks for some time, the group of girls decide to make watches to fit inside the watch boxes provided by the practitioners.

The boys become very interested in the watches at this point and are very pleased to wear the watches which the girls have made for them. Watch faces of different shapes are made, the numerals and pointers are added and watch straps are measured for a perfect fit.

Throughout the next week the children continue to be fascinated by clocks and telling the time. The collection of time related items in the nursery grows as staff, children and parents add old clocks, watches, pictures of clocks, timetables and calendars.

The practitioners decide to make use of the opportunities provided in the local environment to support the children's interests by arranging a visit to a local jeweller's and watchmaker's. As they look in the shop window the children are astonished to see so many different timepieces all in the same place. They begin to count how many clocks they can find and try to work out what time they arrived at the shop.

Once inside the shop the children are delighted by the variety of clocks they see. Their attention is completely focussed as they observe the different faces and decipher the different types of numeral on each clock.

The children look closely at the clocks and talk quietly about the similarities and differences between the clocks and about their personal preferences. They speculate about how old the clocks are.

The wall clocks of differing sizes prompt discussions about which ones the children would hang in their bedrooms – whether or not they are too big, too small or too noisy.

Most surprising of all to the children are the grandfather and grandmother clocks. They ask the practitioners to take photographs of them standing next to the clocks so that they can see how tall the clocks are when they get back to the nursery.

When the children see a wall filled with barometers they are curious to know what they are and what, and how, they measure. The practitioners can see that a whole new investigation is about to begin building on the children's new found interest.

Other things to try

- Make a timeline of a day in the nursery using photographs, accompanied by the time shown on different types of clock face.

- Provide a weatherproof clock in the outdoor area so that children are aware of the passing of time during the day.

- Create a 'museum' of old watches and clocks which you and the children collect. Make labels for each of the exhibits, a guide book with opening and closing times and tickets.

- Play outdoor games such as 'What's the time Mr Wolf?'

Understanding the World outdoors

An environment for Understanding the World

In the EYFS

The following statements are taken from the Learning and Development requirements of the EYFS, Understanding the World.

Understanding the World involves guiding children to make sense of their physical world and their community by providing opportunities to:

- explore
- observe
- find out about people, places, technology and the environment.

Starting points

Thousands of practitioners in the UK have visited the 'Hundred Languages of Children' exhibition from Reggio Emilia which shows the wonderful possibilities of interesting projects based upon children's interests, ideas and theories. Back in their settings, many of these practitioners have developed their learning environments, both indoors and outside, to make it possible to capitalise on the children's curiosity while at the same time providing meaningful opportunities to extend their skills, knowledge and understanding about the world.

Starting points for projects in these settings come from:

- ideas the children develop when they are exploring and investigating.
- situations or events which arise spontaneously in the course of the day.
- suggestions which the practitioners make and then discuss with the children.

Learning and development

Along with many other early years settings in the UK, a nursery in the south of England provides the children with regular Forest School experiences in a local woodland. The practitioners make use of the wider outdoor environment to offer the children starting points for activities which arouse their interest and curiosity.

The children are intrigued by how fallen and felled trees create pathways and 'secret places' in the woodland area. They speculate what might have happened to the trees, about who placed them in position and what might be hiding in the created places.

On the short ride back to the nursery in the mini-bus the children talk about how they could create some places to explore in the nursery garden using the branches, sticks and leaves. In the afternoon, a group of children talk about their plans for creating a mini woodland environment in the garden. They decide that the first thing they need to do is to collect the materials they need from the different areas of the garden.

There is much discussion about how the base of their proposed structure should be created to ensure that it is stable and accessible – both to wildlife and to themselves.

As the twig and stick structure grows the children pose questions such as

'What would happen if we added longer sticks?'
'Can we camouflage the area by adding leaves?'

'Can we find a way to make the structure taller?'
'What can we do to make sure the long sticks don't fall over?'

A second group of children are interested in discovering what they can see underneath the trees in the garden. This interest was sparked by the effects of the sunlight shining through the tree canopy in the woodland earlier in the day.

They decide to draw what they can see above them when they look up through the branches and leaves of the garden trees. Looking up, rather than looking down or straight ahead, gives the children an entirely new perspective on the world outside.

"The practitioners make use of the wider outdoor environment to offer the children starting points for activities which arouse their interest and curiosity."

As the two groups of children are building on their ideas and testing their theories the practitioners record their discussions, to use later in the day to remind the children of what they were doing and thinking. They encourage the children to use the photographs to tell the other members of the larger group what they did, what they found out and what they think might happen next.

From this discussion the practitioners are able to identify what experiences they might provide next in the outdoor environment to build on the children's knowledge, skills, interests and fascinations.

Other things to try

- Use a visit to a local park as a starting point if your setting is unable to access a woodland area.

- Encourage the children to look closely at the trees in your local area regularly throughout the year. This will help them to develop an understanding of how things change over time.

- Use natural materials such as twigs, leaves, conkers, stones and cones for placing and arranging out of doors.

- Take photographs of features in your outdoor area from unusual angles and ask the children to identify them.

Looking closely at living things

In the EYFS

The following statements are taken from the Learning and Development requirements of the EYFS, Understanding the World (The World).

● Children show an interest in aspects of their familiar world.

● They can talk about some of the things they have observed such as plants and animals.

● Children can make observations of animals and plants, and explain why some things occur and talk about changes.

● Children know that the environment and living things are influenced by human activity.

Starting points

In the pre-school section of a large day nursery the children are encouraged to develop their skills of enquiry by practitioners, who are willing to support children as they take risks with their ideas and theories about the world and how it works.

The outdoor area is seen as an environment for curiosity and the children are supported in their investigations by the provision of a wide range of resources which enable them to further their knowledge about living things and their natural habitats.

As part of the nursery's wildlife-friendly garden both a log pile and a rotting tree trunk are found in the outdoor area. This habitat provides food, shelter and a breeding ground for a wide range of small invertebrates.

Learning and development

The children become very excited to find a variety of small creatures inhabiting the rotting tree trunk and they begin to inspect the log regularly to see what they can find.

The practitioners use the opportunity presented by the children's fascination with the spiders, woodlice and insects to help them identify their finds. They encourage the children to look closely at the features of the different invertebrates they find.

They encourage the children to ask:
'Does it have legs?'
If the answer is *'No'* it could be a worm, a slug or a snail.
If the answer is *'Yes'* then ask:
'How many legs does it have?'
If the answer is *'8'* ask: *'Is it a spider?'*
If the answer is *'6'* ask: *'Is it an insect?'*
If the answer is *'14'* ask: *'Is it a woodlouse?'*
If the answer is *'lots'* then it could be a millipede or a centipede.

Building on their interest in the living things in the garden, a group of boys decide that they want to role-play being eco-warriors for the day, following on from discussions about caring for the environment the previous day. They set about collecting together all of the tools and resources they think they will need to create their outdoor laboratory.

When they have familiarised themselves with the magnifiers, Perry's Pooters and collectors' jars and pots, they set of into the undergrowth in the nursery garden to explore.

95

The boys are very excited when they discover several woodlice which they want to study in more depth. They collect the woodlice in a container and take them indoors to investigate. One of the boys asks their key person to help with their enquiry by providing a large sheet of paper and some crayons.

When asked why they need the large sheet of paper the boys reply 'to track the journeys the woodlice make'. They also ask the practitioner to find the camera as they are sure something very interesting is going to happen.

The woodlice are carefully tipped out onto the sheet of paper...

... and the boys begin to track the woodlice as they move around the paper using their crayons.

The woodlice are not entirely co-operative in the boys' attempt to track their journeys which leads to the need for some very urgent solutions and answers to the challenges posed.

One of the boys applies his critical thinking skills to the problem and decides to test his theory that the woodlice could be stopped by the creation of boundaries – he draws a circle around one of the woodlice to prevent it escaping.

The notion of making boundaries is of interest to the other boys and the practitioners are able to build on this interest in many different ways in the coming days.

By documenting the children's learning through a series of photographs the practitioners are able to reflect on the detail of what takes place during the investigation. The images help to make the children's learning and thought processes visible to the practitioners and, later in the day, to their parents.

Other things to try

- During the autumn leaf litter provides an excellent habitat for small invertebrates – this can be investigated both outside and indoors.

- Provide a variety of bird feeders and bird food to attract birds to your outdoor area. Watching the birds will provide endless learning opportunities for the children.

- Buy, or make, nest boxes for birds, bats and hedgehogs.

- Short lengths of bamboo cane tied together will make a 'bug motel' for ladybirds and snails. Woodlice and beetles will live in upturned terracotta pots, airbricks, large stones and piping.

❝In the pre-school section of a large day nursery the children are encouraged to develop their skills of enquiry by practitioners who are willing to support children as they take risks with their ideas and theories about the world and how it works. **❞**

Investigating in the garden

In the EYFS

The following statements are taken from the Learning and Development requirements of the EYFS, Understanding the World (The World).

- Children show an interest in aspects of their familiar world.

- They are curious and interested about why things happen and how things work.

- Children know about similarities and differences in relation to places, objects, materials and living things.

- They can talk about the features of their own immediate environment and how environments might vary from one to another.

Starting points

In a day nursery attended by children from three months to five years of age the owners and practitioners place great value on children learning about growing things and healthy eating.

One of the members of staff has a horticultural background and she shares this expertise with both children and adults. The children have been involved in the design and development of the garden which is an ongoing educational, as well as recreational, project. One of the keys to the success of the children's involvement in the development of the outdoor area is being provided with the right tools for the job.

Learning and development

The toddlers in the nursery enjoy an area of the garden which has been laid out with raised flower and vegetable beds made from wooden sleepers. This means that the beds are at a suitable height for the toddlers to be able to access to enjoy digging and planting.

In late spring in a separate area of the garden the older children make good use of a paved area for growing tomatoes which they will eat later. They use old tyres as planters which adds greenery to an otherwise barren corner of the nursery ground.

The children are accustomed to working collaboratively in the garden and they select their own tools for filling the tyres with soil and compost ...

... before planting out the tomato plants in the tyres. As they work they talk about the plants, what the plants need to survive and how they will need to be cared for.

From a very early age the children are encouraged to look at books to help them find out about plants and living creatures in the garden. In order to do this they need to understand the responsibilities they have when taking books into the garden and then returning them to where they are kept indoors.

During the summer months much interest is shown in the wildlife found in the garden. The children's curiosity is fostered by access to a wide variety of good quality hand lenses and magnifiers. This encourages them to sustain and extend their interest in the natural world.

The practitioners introduce the children to new pieces of equipment and show them how to use the items correctly and safely. Both larger and smaller pieces of equipment are used more effectively by the children when they have observed how to use them and tried them out.

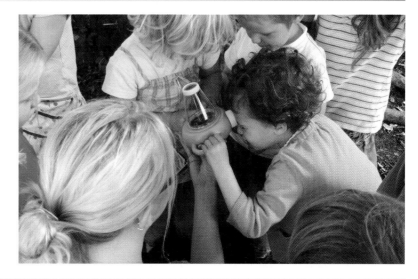

On a daily basis the children collect living things in the garden which they talk about and try to identify. They learn how to handle living things carefully and how best to look at them closely, selecting the right tools for the job in hand.

Wet or cold weather does not deter the children and practitioners from being out of doors in the autumn and winter. The outdoor area offers other opportunities for exploration and investigation. The nursery provides outdoor protective clothing for the children to wear in inclement weather.

Many children will spend sustained periods of time moving things around the outdoor area. Fallen leaves and windfall apples are interesting items to be lifted and transported around the garden using sturdy child-sized wheelbarrows.

More unusual tools such as litter pickers and grabbers involve children in asking themselves questions about how the tools work and what they will do. Introducing more complex tools encourages children to think creatively and to persist when solving challenges.

All year round there are simple tools which children use very effectively as they demonstrate their curiosity about the outdoor environment. The practitioners are aware that two of the most useful tools in the nursery garden are a stick to explore the paths and flowerbeds and a clipboard to record what is found.

Other things to try

- Make an outdoor shadow board for storing tools so that you can see at a glance what has been returned and what is missing.

- Use kitchen tools such as spoons, scoops and small sieves for the youngest children to use in the garden or growing area.

- Brighten up a dull part of the outdoor area by planting climbers and creepers to grow up walls and fences.

- Provide a variety of materials for children to 'lift and shift' around the outdoor area such as logs, stones, pebbles, sand or soil.

Further afield – being part of the community

In the EYFS

The following statements are taken from the Learning and Development requirements of the EYFS, Understanding the World (People and Communities).

- Children can recognise some special times or events in their lives and the lives of others.
- Children know about similarities and differences between themselves and others, and among families, communities and traditions.
- They know that other children don't always enjoy the same things and are sensitive to this.

Starting points

The opening of a new Asian supermarket in a predominantly white area of England provides the opportunity for the practitioners in a nursery to use the wider outdoor environment to help the children begin to gain a meaningful awareness of the cultures of others in their local community.

Two of the children visit the new supermarket with their families and share their experiences with the other children during their group discussion time. The other children in the group express an interest in visiting the new shop and the practitioners agree to arrange a visit.

Learning and development

The practitioners visit the supermarket in advance and agree with the shop owner a good time to visit with the nursery children which is convenient for both parties. The shop owner is delighted by the idea and agrees to visit the nursery briefly beforehand to introduce herself and answer any questions the children might have.

Before they go on their visit the children talk about why they might go to the shop. They decide that they will buy the ingredients for a stir-fry to make when they get back to the nursery. They look through recipe books and make a list of the ingredients they think they will need. Each of the children is responsible for finding one of the ingredients for the stir-fry.

They discuss the route they will take from the nursery and take a simple map along with them to help them find their way.

On arrival at the shop, the children take the opportunity to browse through the different areas, talking about the foods they recognise and those which are new to them. Some of the children are more familiar with the different foods than others and the practitioners encourage them to share their knowledge.

The children then set about locating the specific ingredients which they have come to buy for the stir-fry. Some of the group are sufficiently confident to select the items independently choosing items from the cold store, free-standing baskets and from the shelves. They talk interestedly about the different foods they see and speculate what they are and what they might be used for.

Other children need a little more support from the practitioners as they make their selections. They talk to the children about their choices and explain what the various items in the shop are and how they might be used.

When the children join the queue to pay for their goods, the shop owner talks to them about their purchases and what they are going to cook. She tells them about her favourite foods and the ways in which she cooks them.

The practitioners have ensured that the children can act independently by giving them the money to pay for their purchases. Once again the shop owner talks to them about what she is doing in her work – recording what has been bought, working out the cost and using the till to store money and give the correct change. In this way the children are able to learn about not only foods and customs of other cultures but also about the world of work.

In addition to the different food items in the shop, the children are interested in the signs, notices, posters and labels which have Chinese symbols on them. They ask the shop keeper what the symbols represent and she explains what they mean and how they are formed. Both the children and the practitioners enjoy the opportunity to speak to the shopkeeper and to hear about her life experiences.

When they return to the nursery some of the children decide that they would like to make posters to advertise their Chinese picnic. The practitioners help them find examples of Chinese writing on the internet which they print off and take to their studio area. They choose the brushes they think will be best for the job and create their picnic posters.

The rest of the group of children work with the practitioners to make the stir-fry for the Chinese picnic which is to be held out of doors. As they sample the food, the children are faced with the challenge of using the appropriate utensils to eat with. Some of the children very quickly develop a technique for using the chopsticks very quickly ...

... whereas others need time, and perseverance, to master the physical challenges. All of the children are determined to find their own solutions to eating the meal they have shopped for and prepared.

By placing the visit to the Asian supermarket in the context of becoming familiar with the local community, the practitioners have made the experience of sampling food from another culture a very meaningful experience for the children.

Other things to try

- Take photographs along the route of your journey to a shop and help the children to produce a pictorial map of the journey.

- Go on a visit to shops which sell a variety of breads for the children to try. Include pitta, ciabatta, chapatti, croissant and soda bread.

- Visit a local garden centre and buy packets of fast growing seeds to grow salads, vegetables and flowers in your outdoor area.

- Talk to the children about where different foods come from. Arrange a visit to a local farm or allotment.

“In this way the children are able to learn about not only foods and customs of other cultures but also about the world of work.**”**

Expressive Arts and Design

In the EYFS

The following statements are taken from the Learning and Development requirements of the EYFS, Expressive Arts and Design.

- Children use and explore a variety of materials, experimenting with colour, design, texture, shape and form.

- Children use what they have learned about media and materials in purposeful and original ways.

- They represent their own ideas, thoughts and feelings, through art and design, music, dance, role play and stories.

Starting points

A large day nursery which has taken much of its inspiration from the Reggio Approach to early childhood has appointed a practising artist as a member of staff to work within the nursery, supporting the adults working with all the age groups.

Both indoor and outdoor spaces and the projects which happen are planned by the practitioners and artist to support the children's creativity and creative development. Emphasis is placed upon using the outdoor environment to provide opportunities for creative development on a large scale.

A Montessori nursery also places great emphasis on fostering children's creativity and expressive skills and prioritises opportunities for children to work creatively out of doors.

Learning and development

The older toddlers at the day nursery enjoy playing in the full-sized rowing boat which is a feature of the nursery garden. They talk about making a giant picture of a boat in the outdoor area. The practitioners encourage them to find the materials they might use to represent the boat and together they create the image of the boat outside. One of the practitioners returns to the toddler's home base on the first floor of the nursery and takes a photograph of the artists to remind them of the boat after it has been cleared away at the end of the day.

The pre-school children in the nursery also enjoy the experience of painting out of doors on a large scale. A temporary painting area is regularly created on the patio using plastic sheeting and large sheets or rolls of paper. A variety of brushes are offered and the children mix the paint in small buckets.

The children work collaboratively on group paintings as they explore colour, texture, movement and space. The nursery uses large T-shirts to protect the children's clothing rather than the traditional plastic aprons which the children find restrictive.

Child-initiated learning often takes place outside based on more focussed activities, such as weaving, which have taken place indoors at an earlier date. The children are accustomed to using metal framed weaving frames to design and make patterns and pictures and these are displayed both indoors and outside.

The day after the children have been working on weaving frames indoors a group of children decide to use features of the outdoor environment to practise their new found skills on a large scale. They use lengths of fabric and scarves and weave them through the picket fence surrounding the wooden playhouse.

In another part of the outdoor area a large blackboard is fixed to the rear wall of the building. The children spend the morning drawing on the blackboard with chalks and then they decide to see what happens when they paint with water onto the chalky surface, expressing their artistic thoughts in a different way.

The children are fascinated by the way in which the medium of chalk changes when they paint with water on top of it. They talk about the effects they are creating and about what happens when the water evaporates. The practitioners capture the transient images created by the children as they paint and write their names on the chalky blackboard.

In the Montessori nursery the children explore the effects of using water out of doors in different ways, including spraying water patterns on a wall and creating designs with water and different sized rollers.

During the summer a group of girls become fascinated by designing and creating special places using the many different types of construction materials and fabrics which are accessible to them. They play happily alongside their friends as they work to create the perfect place for their role play.

The girls create an elaborate structure with all the features they need to develop the role play narratives which interest them, ranging from a camping holiday to having friends to stay for a sleepover.

Having ready access to a rich variety of resources in the outdoor environment enables the children to imagine what they want to do, to design their special place and to carry out their plans when their interest is at its height.

Other things to try

- Encourage mark making with clay and mud by the youngest children.

- Use the outdoor area to draw children's attention to the beauty in nature. Encourage them to take photographs of beautiful things they see.

- Have music, ribbons and streamers available outdoors so that children can enjoy dance and movement in a large space.

- Play musical instruments outdoors – a higher level of sound is likely to be more tolerable than indoors.

Music, movement and dance outside

In the EYFS

The following statements are taken from the Learning and Development requirements of the EYFS, Expressive Arts and Design (Exploring using media and materials).

- Children imitate and create movement in response to music and join in dancing games.

- They sing to themselves, explore sounds, and tap out simple repeated rhythms.

- Children sing songs, make music and dance and experiment with ways of changing them.

Starting points

In a children's centre the practitioners invite a wide range of practising artists, including musicians, dancers, story tellers and visual artists, to extend the children's experiences and to support the professional development of the staff.

The children's centre staff organise creative arts days for children, parents and families from the local neighbourhood.

Learning and development

Music making and dancing out of doors brings a whole new dimension to the children's learning and development. Instruments can be used out of doors to accompany both singing games and dancing.

Being outside often means that instruments which make louder noises can be played without disturbing children and adults in other parts of the outdoor area.

The outdoor area of the children's centre includes some large scale musical instruments which are available to be played by the children at all times.

With funding obtained for a music project which involves practising musicians working in early years settings, the staff of the children's centre and a local musician design and build a large scale tuned xylophone for the outdoor area. This enables the children to explore how sounds are made and changed and to begin to create music themselves.

Good use is made of the musical potential of the wooden climbing frame in the outdoor play area. The artist working with the children's centre has created a musical instrument using different lengths of drain pipe secured under the wooden frame. The pipes are cut to the correct length to ensure that the musical instrument is tuned.

In order to play the instrument the player runs from one part of the instrument to another, hitting the end of the pipes with a table tennis bat to make the various sounds. This is an experience which appeals particularly to the boys who enjoy making music whilst being active and on the move.

The outdoor area of any early years setting provides the perfect opportunity for the children to explore sound, rhythm and movement. Playing music out of doors for the children to move to, along with streamers and ribbons, encourages both boys and girls to move rhythmically and to match their movements to music.

Being out of doors means that the children can practise using large movements, experiencing the joy of dancing and singing in a less confined space than they have available indoors.

Other things to try

- Provide a 'pots and pans' band for the very youngest children to play out of doors.

- Use drums to accompany marching songs such as 'The Grand old Duke of York.'

- Listen to the sounds which can be heard in your outdoor area and encourage the children to reproduce the sounds using musical instruments.

- Make an outdoor organ by securing lengths of pipe(which have U-bends at the bottom) to a fence or wall. Use a table tennis bat or flip-flop to strike the tops of the tubes to make the sound.

Placing and arranging in the natural world

In the EYFS

The following statements are taken from the Learning and Development requirements of the EYFS, Expressive Arts and Design (Exploring and using media and materials, Being Imaginative).

- Children create simple representations of events, people and objects.

- They use and explore a variety of materials, experimenting with colour, design, texture, shape and form.

- Children use what they have learned about media and materials in purposeful and original ways.

- They can talk about features of their own and others' work, recognising the differences between them and the strengths of each.

Starting points

In a day nursery the staff and children have a long term interest in the work of the artist Andy Goldsworthy and they use images of his work to inspire the children's learning and development. Andy Goldsworthy is a sculptor and photographer who uses a wide range of natural materials – including brightly coloured flowers, icicles, mud, pine cones, snow, stone and twigs – in his transient art in both natural and urban settings.

Learning and development

The practitioners and children in the pre-school group in the nursery look at books about the work of Andy Goldsworthy. As it is autumn they are particularly interested in the images of arrangements which show autumn leaves and fruits.

The children use a wide range of materials, both indoors and outside, to express and communicate their ideas and feelings, on both a small and a large scale.

Two of the children set off around the garden using their lightweight collapsible collectors' buckets to forage for the natural materials which are available. First they collect fallen fruit and dead flower heads from the flowerbeds.

Then they move into the centre of the garden to collect leaves, twigs, conkers and dried grass as the materials they will use to create their natural sculptures.

Often the children create their arrangements directly onto the grass or outdoor paved area within the setting. However, on this occasion, they state their preference for using a white builders' tray as their blank canvas. They gently tip their natural treasures on to the surface of the tray, looking closely at some of the individual items and beginning to think how they will use them.

The children talk about their ideas, negotiating which of the ideas they will use in their work. They respond to comments and questions from their friends and show equal enthusiasm for developing other ideas as well as their own. They focus for a sustained period of time on achieving a result which is pleasing to all of them.

The practitioners encourage the children to take photographs of their creations, partly so that they have a record of their transient art but also so that they can reflect on their ideas later and share their thoughts with the rest of the children and with their families at the end of the day. By documenting the children's learning processes the practitioners can build on their interests and fascinations.

Other things to try

- Take note of which children prefer to respond to experiences and express their ideas by placing and arranging and provide other opportunities for them to do so.

- Use a variety of outdoor surfaces for the children to use for placing and arranging – on grass, on a tree trunk, on paving or on a muddy area.

- Create a storage area in the outdoor environment to house materials and resources, natural and manmade, for placing and arranging.

- Take note of how children use 'found' materials in the natural environment to represent other objects in the course of their play.

Further afield – working with the community

In the EYFS

The following statements are taken from the Learning and Development requirements of the EYFS, Expressive Arts and Design (Exploring media and materials, Being imaginative).

- Children explore and differentiate between colours and begin to describe the texture of things.

- They use and explore a variety of materials, experimenting with colour, design, texture, shape and form.

- Children talk about the ideas and processes which have led them to make design designs, images or products.

- Through their explorations they find out, and make decisions about, how media and materials can be combined and changed.

Starting points

A day nursery in the south of England is involved in the local community's open house days for artists and makers where members of the public are invited into a range of diverse spaces to view their work.

Shortly after the nursery opened, the owners decided that they would welcome the local community into the nursery by involving the children and families in exhibiting the children's work.

Learning and development

By becoming involved in the local artists' open house weekends the nursery has established itself as part of the local community with children of all ages creating their own works of art, which are worthy of being exhibited. The practitioners talk to the older children about the artists' open house weekend and ask whether or not they think the nursery should become involved.

The children have become interested in the work of a range of artists whom they have found out about during a long term exploration of colour. They are particularly fascinated by the work of Pollock and Rothko and decide that it would be a good idea to model their exhibition on the work of these two artists.

Having looked closely at the work of the artists in books and on the internet, the children decide that the older members of the nursery should focus on Rothko whilst the paintings of Pollock might inspire the whole nursery.

Having experimented with different painting techniques, the children agree that the 'Pollock paintings' will be created out of doors. They begin by experimenting on large sheets of paper attached to the outer wall of the nursery before deciding, as a group, that a specially prepared painting area should be created on the nursery patio.

The babies and toddlers experience 'splash' painting on a small scale indoors before being given the opportunity to create their individual and group canvases in the outdoor studio space.

They choose to stand, kneel or sit to complete their paintings and are inventive in their choice of brushes and the other tools which they choose to use to make marks on the canvases.

The three year olds focus on exploring the different colours and on the effects of their movements on the end result. They talk about the different patterns they are making and enjoy imitating each other's movements as they paint.

The pre-school children refer to the work of Pollock before they start work on their finished canvases. They are engrossed in their creative expression and are confident in representing their ideas.

The children have very clear ideas about the colours they want to use and the effects they want to create. They make precise movements with their brushes to create the effects they have in mind and carefully mix the exact colours they want to use.

During the artists' open house weekend the canvases are displayed by the practitioners in the form of an exhibition in a gallery. Each of the paintings is carefully displayed showing the children's names and ages and the title given by the 'artist' where appropriate.

The exhibition is included in the open house weekend programme under the title 'Reflections on Rothko and Pollock'. The nursery is visited by large numbers of the general public as well as by the families of the artists themselves.

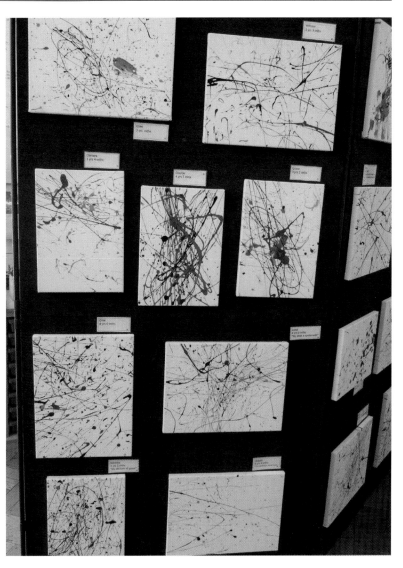

The canvases are sold to raise funds to pay for the building of a nursery in Africa, with the families being invited to purchase their children's work at the gallery preview.

Those which are not sold remain in the nursery and are hung in several of the indoor spaces, including the staircase and nappy changing area, to create a beautiful environment.

Using the outdoor environment to its full advantage enables the staff and owners of the nursery to showcase the wonderful creations of the children on a scale which would not be possible if creative development were to be limited to the indoors.

Other things to try

- Explore the possibilities of having an artist work with the children in your setting. Ensure that the artist is familiar with working with children in the early years.

- Ask the local library, shop or church if they would be willing to host an exhibition of your children's artwork.

- Use frames and mounts from a local picture framing shop to give value to the children's paintings.

- Cover paintings with a PVA glue glaze and hang them in the outdoor environment.

❝ The nursery has established itself as part of the local community with children of all ages creating their own works of art which are worthy of being exhibited. ❞

Books and other resources

Books and publications

The Little Book of Living Things, Linda Thornton and Pat Brunton (2005) Featherstone Education

The Little Book of Time and Place, Linda Thornton and Pat Brunton (2004) Featherstone Education

Understanding the Reggio Approach (2nd edition) Linda Thornton and Pat Brunton (2009) Routledge

Bringing the Reggio Approach to Your Early Years Practice (2nd edition) Linda Thornton and Pat Brunton (2010) Routledge

Playing and Learning Outdoors, Jan White (2007) Routledge

Outdoor Provision in the Early Years Jan White (ed) (2011) Sage

Forest Schools and Outdoor Learning in the Early Years, Sara Knight (2009) Sage

Risk and Adventure in Early Years Outdoor Play, Sara Knight (2011) Sage

Resources

Reflections on Learning sell a wide range of resources to support active play and learning out of doors, including magnifiers, sand and water resources, gardening tools and equipment, waterproof clothing, outdoor seating, tents and dens. www.reflectionsonlearning.co.uk, 01732 225850.

Learning through Landscapes provides training and resources to support practitioners develop their outdoor provision. www.ltl.org.uk

Archimedes Training run training courses and have a wide range of resources of interest to practitioners wanting to know more about the Forest Schools Approach. www.forestschools.com